Flipperrific Big Book Of Big Fish (Whales, Dolphins etc)

Speedy Publishing LLC
40 E. Main St. #1156
Newark, DE 19711

www.speedypublishing.com

Copyright 2014
9781635012095
First Printed November 5, 2014

All Rights reserved. No part of this book may be reproduced or used in any way or form or by any means whether electronic or mechanical, this means that you cannot record or photocopy any material ideas or tips that are provided in this book.

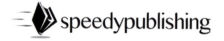

Did you know?

Compared to other animals, dolphins are believed to be very intelligent.

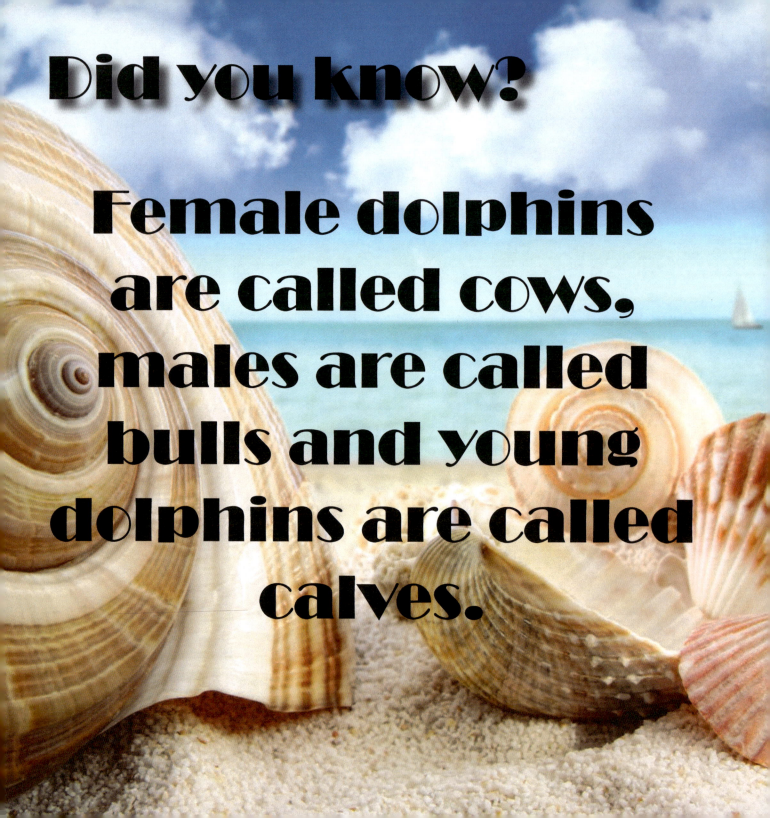

Did you know?

Dolphins often display a playful attitude which makes them popular in human culture. They can be seen jumping out of the water, riding waves, play fighting and occasionally interacting with humans swimming in the water.

Did you know? The Killer Whale (also known as Orca) is actually a type of dolphin.

Did you know?

Dolphins are carnivores (meat eaters). Dolphins live in schools or pods of up to 12 individuals.

Did you know?

Also known as "sea canaries," belugas are one of the most the most vocal of all whales.

Did you know?

Sharks do not have a single bone in their bodies. Instead they have a skeleton made up of cartilage; the same type of tough, flexible tissue that makes up human ears and noses.

Did you know?

Great whites are the deadliest shark in the ocean. These powerful predators can race through the water at 30 km per hour.

Did you know?

The humpback has a distinctive body shape, with unusually long pectoral fins and a knobbly head. An acrobatic animal known for breaching and slapping the water with its tail and pectorals, it is popular with whale watchers off the coasts of Australasia and the Americas.

Did you know?

Found in oceans and seas around the world, humpback whales typically migrate up to 25,000 kilometres (16,000 mi) each year. Humpbacks feed only in summer, in polar waters, and migrate to tropical or subtropical waters to breed and give birth in the winter.

Did you know?

Giant manta rays reach up to around 7m in width compared to reef mantas, which grow to around 5m in width and can travel 70km in a single day.

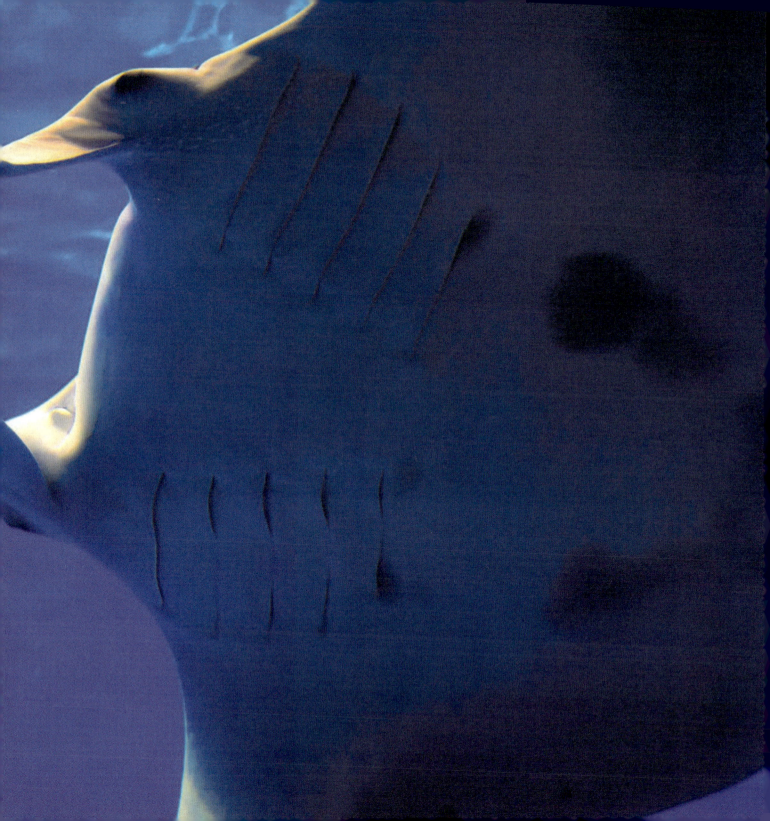

Did you know?

Whale sharks are the largest fish on the planet. Whale sharks are in no way related to whales. Although they are sharks, they are very docile and pose no real threats to humans.

Did you know?

Whale sharks can reach up to 14m (46 feet!) in length. Whale sharks can weigh up to 12 tons. That's 24,000 pounds or nearly 11,000 kilos!!

Did you know?

A baby whale is called a calf. Whales form groups to look after calves and feed together. These groups are often made up of all female or all male whales.

Did you know?

In 2009, a captive beluga whale rescued a distressed participant of a free diving competition by pushing her to the surface.

Did you know?

There are 79 to 84 different species of whale. They came in many different shapes and sizes! You can tell the age of a whale by looking at the wax plug in its ear.

Did you know?

Whales love to sing! They use this as a call to mates, a way to communicate and also just for fun! After a period of time they get bored of the same whale song and begin to sing a different tune.

Did you know?

Orcas are highly social animals that travel in groups called pods. Pods usually consist of 5 to 30 whales, although some pods may combine to form a group of 100 or more.

Did you know?

Orcas establish social hierarchies, and pods are lead by females. The animals are thought to have a complex form of communication with different dialects from one pod to another.

Made in the USA
Lexington, KY
17 May 2016